Tough Topics

Death

Patricia J. Murphy

Heinemann Library
Chicago, Illinois

Photo research by Erica Martin
Designed by Richard Parker and Q2A Creative
Printed and bound in China by South China Printing Company

09 08 07
10 9 8 7 6 5 4 3 2 1

Library of Congress Cataloging-in-Publication Data
  Murphy, Patricia J., 1963-
  Death / Patricia J. Murphy.
  p. cm. -- (Tough topics)
  Includes index.
  ISBN 978-1-4034-9778-9 (hardback) -- ISBN 978-1-4034-9783-3 (pbk.)
  1. Death--Juvenile literature. 2. Bereavement--Juvenile literature. I. Title.
  HQ1073.3.M87 2007
  155.9'37--dc22

                         2007007230

Acknowledgments
The publishers would like to thank the following for permission to reproduce photographs:
© Alamy pp. **18** (Bubbles Photolibrary), **20** (Imagebroker), **21** (PhotoAlto), **22** (BananaStock); © Corbis pp. **13** (Jutta Klee), **24** (LWA-Dann Tardif), **26** (Randy Faris), **29** (Jose Luis Pelaez, Inc.); © Getty Images pp. **4** (Paul Chesley), **5** (Steffen Thalemann), **6** (Chad Slattery), **8** (Ghislain & Marie David de Lossy), **9** (Juan Silva), **11** (Michael Malyszko), **15** (Meg Takamura), **19** (Photodisc); © Jupiter Images p. **7** (Rubberball); © Masterfile pp. **12** (Matthew Plexman), **23** (Masterfile www.masterfile.com); © Photoedit p. **14** (David Young-Wolff); © Photolibrary pp. **16** (SW Productions), **17** (Banana Stock), **27** (Imagesource); © Photolibrary.Com p. **28**; © Rex Features pp. **10** (Gustafsson), **25** (Voisin / Phanie)

Cover photograph of tombstone reproduced with permission of © Corbis (Zefa/ Ole Graf).

Every effort has been made to contact copyright holders of any material reproduced in this book. Any omissions will be rectified in subsequent printings if notice is given to the publisher.

Contents

Some words are shown in bold, **like this**. You can find out what they mean by looking in the Glossary.

What Is Death?

All living things go through stages. They are born, they live, and they die. Death is the end of life.

▲ All living things will die one day.

Plants and animals die. People die, too. Most people will live a long life before they do.

Why Do People Die?

▲ People can die suddenly, such as in a car accident.

Some people may die after they have been very sick. Others may have been injured so badly that their bodies cannot work to stay alive.

Often times, people die because they are very old. They die of **natural causes** or of old age.

▲ Some people may die after a long illness.

Saying Goodbye

Sometimes, people die suddenly and sometimes slowly. Some people may have time to say goodbye to their loved ones before they die.

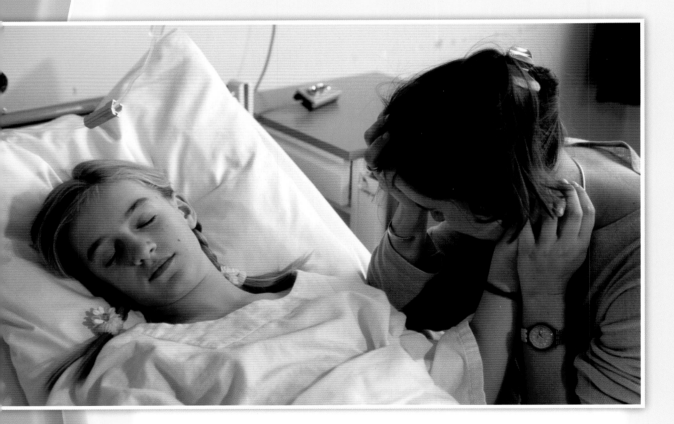

▲ If a loved one has been sick for a long time, you may have a chance to visit and say goodbye.

▲ It can be a great shock when a loved one dies suddenly.

Other times, people do not get a chance to say goodbye to their loved one before he or she dies. This is because their loved one may have died very suddenly.

Celebrating a Life

When a loved one dies, a family may have a **funeral** or a similar **ceremony** for them. A funeral is a time to celebrate the life of the person who has died.

▶Some people are buried in a coffin.

At a funeral, there may be a **service**, prayers, music, and speeches. People speak about how their loved one lived and say their last goodbyes.

After the Funeral

◄ You can visit the place where a loved one is buried in a cemetery.

After the **funeral**, people may go to a **cemetery** to bury the body of their loved one. Other times, the ashes of the loved one may be placed in a container called an **urn**. Sometimes, people go to their loved one's favorite place to spread these ashes.

After the **burial**, there may be a **reception** or gathering. A reception is usually at a family member's home. At the reception, people may share a meal together. Often times, they also say how sorry they are for the family's loss and offer comfort or help.

Grieving

When people lose a loved one, they often **grieve**. To grieve is to feel very sad. People who grieve may not want to believe that their loved one is dead. They might have trouble accepting that their loved one will not be there to talk to or share special moments.

No two people grieve in the same way. Some people may grieve for a long period or for a short while. Either way, one day their grief will fade away. In its place will be **memories** of the person they lost.

Feeling Guilty

Often people feel **guilt** when they lose a loved one. You may feel guilty if you did not get to say goodbye to your loved one.

▲ You may remember arguments you had with your loved one and feel guilty about them.

▶ Looking at photographs of your loved one can help you talk about your feelings.

Writing a letter to your **deceased** loved one may help you deal with these feelings. Sharing your feelings with a family member or friends may also help you feel better.

Feeling Sad

◄ If you have lost a loved one, it is important to cry if you need to.

Most people feel a deep sadness when a loved one dies. They may feel sad that they cannot spend time with them anymore. They may also cry when they think about their loved one.

After a while, these sad feelings will go away. If you feel sad for a long time, talk to a **counselor** or trusted adult. They will be able to help you.

▶ Sharing your feelings with others may help you.

Feeling Angry

Some people might feel angry about a loved one's death. You might wonder why your loved one had to die and think that it is unfair. Your angry feelings might make you want to yell.

▲ Never take your anger out on other people.

▲ Talking about your angry feelings with other people can help.

Feeling angry is okay as long as you do not act badly towards others. When you feel angry, do something that helps you calm down. You could take a walk or play basketball.

Feeling Lonely

▲ You may think that other people do not understand how you are feeling.

Soon after a loved one has died, you may feel **lonely**. You may miss seeing your loved one.

To feel less lonely, you could spend more time with other family members and friends doing things that you enjoy. You may also find new friends and new things to do.

Getting Help

Losing a loved one changes your life. This loss can leave you with many sad feelings. It is important that you share these feelings with someone who listens well.

◄ Grief counselors help people deal with grief in healthy ways and accept the loss of loved ones.

You could turn to family members, friends, or a teacher for help. If these people are not able to help, you might want to talk to a **grief counselor**.

Missing a Loved One

When a loved one dies, it is normal to miss them. You may wish that your loved one was still part of your daily life.

▲ You might think of your loved one on special days, such as holidays and birthdays.

You might find it helpful to keep your loved one's **memory** alive. You can do this by remembering the special things about them, and the times you shared together.

Remembering a Loved One

There are many ways people can remember their loved ones. You could keep your favorite pictures of them around or make a scrapbook about them.

▲ You could plant a tree in your loved one's memory.

You could write stories to share **memories** about your loved one. If you surround yourself with these things, you will keep your loved one's memory close to you. While things will be different without your loved one, life will go on.

Ways to Cope With Grief

- Write your feelings in a journal.

- Draw or paint a picture of you and your loved one and hang it up where you can see it.

- Do something that you and your loved one enjoyed doing together. Think about your loved one while you are doing it.

- Give yourself all the time you need to fully **grieve** the loss of your loved one. Then, take it one day at a time.

- Remember that even though your loved one has died, you will always have the love that you shared. Love never dies.

Glossary

burial event when a body is put into the ground

cemetery place where dead people are buried and remembered

ceremony actions, words, and music performed to mark an important day

counselor person trained to give advice

deceased not alive; dead

funeral ceremony held after someone has died

grief feeling of great sadness when someone you love has died

guilt feeling bad for having done something wrong

lonely feeling all alone

natural causes normal reasons

reception gathering for a special occasion. A reception often follows a funeral or special ceremony.

service special ceremony

urn special vase used to store the ashes of someone who has died

More Books to Read

Latta, Sara. *Dealing with the Loss of a Loved One*. Philadelphia, PA: Chelsea House, 2003.

Royston, Angela. *Living and Nonliving*. Chicago, IL: Heinemann Library, 2003.

Ruiz, Ruth Ann. *Coping with the Death of a Brother or Sister*. New York: Rosen, 2001.

Thomas, Pat. *I Miss You: A First Look at Death*. Hauppauge, N.Y: Barron's Educational Series, 2001.

Index